What's THe DeAl?

Smoking

www.heinemann.co.uk/library

Visit our website to find out more information about Heinemann Library books.

To order:
☎ Phone 44 (0) 1865 888066
▤ Send a fax to 44 (0) 1865 314091
▢ Visit the Heinemann Bookshop at www.heinemann.co.uk/library to browse
our catalogue and order online.

Produced for Heinemann Library by
White-Thomson Publishing Ltd,
Bridgewater Business Centre,
210 High Street, Lewes,
East Sussex, BN7 2NH.

First published in Great Britain by Heinemann Library,
Jordan Hill, Oxford OX2 8EJ, part of Harcourt Education.

Heinemann Library is a registered trademark of
Harcourt Education Ltd.

Consultant: Jenny McWhirter, Head of Education and
    Prevention, DrugScope
Editorial: Clare Collinson
Design: Tim Mayer
Picture Research: Elaine Fuoco-Lang and Amy Sparks
Production: Duncan Gilbert

Originated by P.T. Repro Multi Warna
Printed and bound in China, by South China
    Printing Company.

The paper used to print this book comes from
sustainable resources.

The case studies and quotations in this book are
based on factual examples. However, in some cases,
the names or other personal information have been
changed to protect the privacy of the individual
concerned.

10 digit ISBN 0 431 10784 X (hardback)
13 digit ISBN 978 0 431 10784 4 (hardback)
10 09 08 07 06
10 9 8 7 6 5 4 3 2 1

10 digit ISBN 0 431 10796 3 (paperback)
13 digit ISBN 978 0 431 10796 7 (paperback)
11 10 09 08 07
10 9 8 7 6 5 4 3 2 1

British Library Cataloguing in Publication Data
Bingham, Jane
    Smoking. – (What's the deal?)
    1. Smoking – Juvenile literature. 2. Tobacco habit –
    Juvenile literature
    I. Title
    362.2'96
A full catalogue record for this book is available from
the British Library.

Acknowledgements
The publisher would like to thank the following for
their kind permission to use their photographs:

Alamy Images **4** (Ace Stock Limited), **5** (Mark
Baigent), **9** (Medical-on-Line), **23** (PS/DW), **28** (Ansell
Horn/Phototake Inc), **32** (Photofusion Picture
Library/George Montgomery), **35** (Janine Wiedel
Photolibrary), **44** (Iain Masterton); Corbis **6** (Bob
Rowan/Progressive Image), **12** (Baumgartner
Olivia/Corbis Sygma), **13** (Jose Luis Pelaez Inc), **16–17**
(Bill Varie), **25** (Gabe Palmer), **27** (Health Promotion
Board/Reuters), **30** (Ronnie Kaufman), **31**, **46**
(Reza/Webistan), **48** (Steve Sands/New York
Newswire), **50** (Reed Kaestner); Rex Features **7** (A
Nordahl), **10** (Action Press), **11** (Everett Collection),
22 (Voisin/Phanie), **26** (Alix/Phanie), **29** (Richard
Young), **39** (Voisin/Phanie), **40** (Voisin/Phanie);
Science Photo Library **9** (Matt Meadows, Peter
Arnold Inc); Topfoto **8** (Drew Farrell), **14**, **19** (Iain
Brown), **20–21** (The Image Works), **24** (The Image
Works), **33**, **36–37** (The Image Works), **42–43** (The
Image Works).

Cover artwork by Phil Weyman, Kralinator Design.

Every effort has been made to contact copyright
holders of any material reproduced in this book. Any
omissions will be rectified in subsequent printings if
notice is given to the publishers.

Contents

▌Words appearing in the text in bold, **like this**, are explained in the Glossary.

Half a pack a day for seven years did not seem like heavy smoking to Katherine, who started smoking cigarettes in her last year of university. She believed it gave her a glamorous and sophisticated image. In her mid–twenties Katherine was diagnosed with smoking–induced cancer. At the age of 29 she underwent intensive **radiation therapy** for advanced tongue cancer. For two years after the treatment she could only eat baby food.

Today Katherine is a successful lawyer and a passionate supporter of anti-smoking campaigns. But her life has been permanently affected by smoking. She is very weak and has constant neck pain. Strangers who meet her for the first time don't realize that her slurred speech is the result of her surgery and usually assume that she is drunk.

❚ There's no doubt about it – smoking is a filthy habit.

However, despite all this, Katherine knows she is very lucky to be alive. She is determined that as many young people as possible should learn from what happened to her. "How stupid was I," she asks, "to think that just because I was young, I was not vulnerable to cancer?"

Every year, millions of people like Katherine are forced to face the consequences of smoking. One of those people could be you. What decisions will you make about smoking?

A dangerous habit

What is it about smoking? It gives you a hacking cough, makes you smell disgusting, and costs a small fortune. It causes a terrifying range of diseases and often leads to early death. But, despite these things, billions of people all over the world use tobacco.

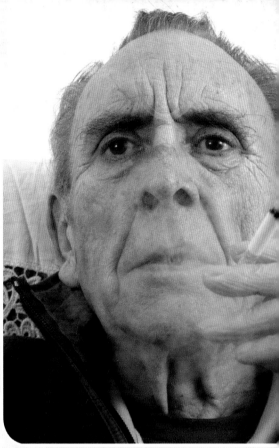

❙ Smoking does nothing for your looks! Heavy smokers end up with grey, wrinkled skin.

Making decisions

You might think that smoking won't be an issue for you. But if you are tempted, or become **addicted**, what will you do? This book gives you the facts you need to make up your own mind about smoking. It looks at why people start smoking, what keeps them smoking, and why they find it so hard to quit. There are also many issues to think about. What part is played by the giant tobacco industry in keeping people hooked on tobacco, and what can be done to make people more aware of the dangers of smoking? Let's look at smoking and the real harm it can do.

⚠ Smoking kills

- Tobacco is the only legally available consumer product that kills people when used normally.

- Smoking causes over 50 diseases and disorders – many of them fatal.

- Half of all long-term smokers are killed by tobacco – losing an average of sixteen years of life.

5

Tobacco is made from the dried leaves of the plant *Nicotiana tabacum*. It is processed into various products, including cigarettes, cigars, pipe tobacco, **chew**, and **snuff** (powdered tobacco for sniffing).

The history of smoking

Over a thousand years ago, some Native Americans discovered that they could dry tobacco leaves and smoke them in a pipe. In the 1500s, European settlers in North America began to smoke too. The Europeans sent dried tobacco back to Europe, and the practice of smoking spread very fast. In the 17th and 18th centuries snuff was fashionable. A trend for cigar smoking followed in the 19th century, but by the 1890s cigarettes had taken over, as the automatic rolling machine was introduced. This machine allowed thousands of cigarettes to be produced in a very short period of time. After World War I (1914–18), there was a huge increase in smoking. It was around this time that the big tobacco companies were formed to take advantage of the growing trend.

❚ Some people smoke hand-rolled cigarettes without a filter, which means they **inhale** more tar than smokers of ordinary cigarettes.

Cigarettes

Today, smoking manufactured cigarettes is the most common way of consuming tobacco. Cigarettes are made from shredded tobacco leaves, paper, and a wide range of **additives**, such as **preservatives** and flavourings. Most cigarettes have a **filter** at the end, which is designed to stop some of the **tar** in cigarette smoke reaching the lungs. Some people buy loose tobacco to make into hand-rolled cigarettes.

▌Cigarette production is very big business. Millions of cigarettes are produced in factories every day.

Oral tobacco

Not all tobacco users smoke cigarettes. In parts of Africa and Asia, people chew dried tobacco leaves mixed with other leaves and spices. In the United States, there is a growing trend among young men to use chew or **dip** tobacco. Dip users take a pinch or "dip" of tobacco and place a wad in their cheek or between their lower lip and gums. This is a very dangerous practice that often results in cancer of the mouth.

Sean's story

For many young users of chew or dip tobacco, cancer can strike very fast. This is Sean's story.

Sean Marsee lived in Ada, Oklahoma. An enthusiastic athlete, he won a total of 28 medals in his short sporting career. Sean began chewing tobacco at the age of twelve. When cancer of the mouth was first detected Sean was eighteen. His tongue was surgically removed, followed by his jawbone. He died one week before his nineteenth birthday.

Did you know that tobacco smoke contains over 4,000 chemicals? These chemicals cause serious damage to smokers' bodies. All forms of tobacco contain **nicotine** – a substance that is poisonous if it is taken in sufficient strength. The nicotine in tobacco is highly **addictive**, so it has the effect of making people want to smoke more.

A poisonous cocktail

It is impossible to list all the chemicals released into a smoker's body when tobacco smoke is **inhaled**. But at least 40 of them are **carcinogens** – substances that have been proved to cause cancer.

▌ Each time smokers inhale, they take at least 40 cancer-causing chemicals into their body.

"One day I decided to give smoking a try ... I wanted to find out what all the fuss was about. My mate passed me a cigarette and I inhaled. The smoke burned my throat and scalded my lungs and it felt like I was choking. I tried it one more time and it was even worse. The smoke tasted foul and I felt sick and dizzy. If that's how smoking makes you feel, I can do without it."

Tom, a non-smoker aged seventeen

⚠ Nicotine facts

- Some scientists claim that nicotine is as addictive as heroin and cocaine.

- In the form of nicotine oil, nicotine is used as a deadly spray to kill insects.

Tar and gas

Smoke from cigarettes contains tiny droplets of a brown, sticky substance called **tar**. When someone inhales tobacco smoke into their lungs, some of the tar droplets **condense** and stick to the inside of their lungs. Gradually, a coating of tar builds up, reducing the lungs' ability to fight off illnesses such as colds, **bronchitis**, and **pneumonia**.

Burning tobacco also creates a gas called **carbon monoxide**. When this gas enters a smoker's bloodstream, it affects the body's ability to deliver oxygen to the tissues and organs of the body. When muscles and organs do not receive enough oxygen, they don't work as well. So smokers find that breathing is more of an effort and exercise makes them feel tired very quickly.

The nicotine trap

Of all the dangerous ingredients in tobacco, the most dangerous of all is nicotine. After just a few cigarettes, nicotine gets people hooked. Nicotine is a mild **stimulant** that acts on the brain, causing it to make chemicals that produce a feeling of pleasure. Many new smokers discover that once they have experienced this sensation, they find themselves wanting it again. You can read more about nicotine addiction on pages 16–17.

Why do people smoke?

Every year, millions of people take up smoking, and the vast majority of these first-time users are under eighteen. But why do people choose to smoke, when there are so many warnings against it?

▌ Sometimes it can seem hard to refuse a friend, but there are plenty of very good reasons to say no to tobacco.

Joining in?

Many young people try their first cigarette just to join in with their mates. Their friends may encourage them to have a cigarette and they may not feel able to say no. They may feel under pressure to behave in a certain way to fit in with the rest of the gang. The pressure doesn't always come from what their friends are saying, but it certainly comes from what they are doing. It is important to remember in a situation like this that people should be free to make their own decisions about smoking. A true friend accepts you as you are.

Looking cool?

Some young people start smoking because they want to be rebellious. They may see smoking as a way of going against authority and looking "hard" and tough. Many others think it makes them look cool, sexy, and sophisticated.

Media images of glamorous people smoking help to reinforce the idea that it's cool to smoke. In a recent survey, over 600 US pupils aged between 10 and 19 answered questions about film stars, such as Leonardo Di Caprio, who regularly smoke on screen. The survey revealed that the more a star smoked, the more attractive smoking appeared to their fans. However, there are things that on-screen smoking just doesn't show. There's nothing glamorous or cool about smelly breath, for example. And many famous film stars have died from smoking-related illnesses.

▌John Wayne was a Hollywood legend who played the tough guy in Westerns and war films. Often shown smoking on screen, Wayne had to have a lung removed because of lung cancer. In his later years, Wayne spoke out against smoking.

Viewpoints

Some people think that film stars who are role models for young people should refuse to take on parts that involve smoking. Other people say this is unrealistic.

● It's irresponsible for stars to smoke on screen

Famous screen stars should realize that many young people are influenced by what they do. If they smoke on screen, young people may think it looks cool and copy them. They should be more responsible and not accept roles that involve smoking.

● Screen stars should be free to do what they like

Actors should be free to accept the roles they want. It's unrealistic to expect them not to smoke if smoking is a part of the character they're playing. People should make up their own mind about smoking, without being influenced by stars – no matter how good looking or famous they are.

What do you think?

Dealing with problems

Many smokers claim that they need their cigarettes to help them relax. They say that smoking allows them to unwind, and also makes them feel calmer about any problems or difficulties in their lives. Unfortunately, smokers find that in fact their habit adds a lot to the stresses of everyday life (see pages 18–19).

"How could I ever have thought that smoking was a sociable habit? What could be more anti-social than breathing disgusting, poisonous fumes into my friends' faces?"

Lee, an ex-smoker

Some smokers also say that smoking helps them to concentrate. They say that having a cigarette while they work allows them to think much more clearly. But this can be a problem too, as most workplaces today operate a ban on smoking. So, instead of finding it easier to concentrate on their work, smokers are distracted by constant **cravings** for a cigarette.

Just a social habit?

People often say that they are just "social" smokers, meaning that they only smoke when they are socializing with friends. They might feel awkward in a social situation, and find that smoking gives them something to do. However, nowadays, many restaurants, cafes, and bars ban smoking altogether, so people have to go outside to smoke, away from their friends. Because tobacco is so **addictive**, it's very easy for a "social" smoking habit to spill over into the rest of someone's life.

❚ Smokers soon start to rely on cigarettes just to get them through the day.

Staying slim?

Some people say that smoking helps them stay slim. **Nicotine** has the effect of suppressing the smoker's appetite. Also, food doesn't taste very good when your mouth and tongue are coated with tobacco smoke. For both these reasons, some heavy smokers tend not to eat properly.

However, many smokers find that they actually put on weight after they start smoking. Smoking makes people breathless and less energetic, so taking exercise becomes much harder. This means it's easy for a smoker to become unfit and overweight.

❚ The best way to look good and stay slim is to eat healthily and do plenty of exercise.

Kate's story

Kate thought of herself as a "social" smoker, who could give up whenever she wanted to. But then she split up with her boyfriend and started smoking more heavily. She kept telling herself she'd cut down soon, but as the months went by she realized it wasn't so easy. Kate was stuck with a serious habit and she wished she'd never started smoking at all.

▋ Tobacco companies often try to link their brands with a certain type of image to persuade people to buy their cigarettes.

The tobacco business

One major reason why so many people smoke is the power of the giant companies that make and sell tobacco. Together, these powerful companies devote millions of pounds each year to persuading the public to buy their products.

Advertising pays

Ever since the early 20th century, tobacco companies have used clever ways to advertise their products and persuade people to smoke. From the 1950s onwards, the companies spent a fortune on advertisements in magazines, on TV, in the cinema, and on huge **billboards**. No one could get away from tempting images of their products.

Most of the early tobacco advertisements showed attractive people in glamorous surroundings enjoying a cigarette. Even in the 1970s, when there was mounting evidence that smoking seriously damaged people's health, tobacco companies still continued to promote smoking as part of a fun, active, and healthy lifestyle.

Today, some forms of tobacco advertising, such as billboards and TV adverts, are illegal in many countries. But the tobacco industry still finds ways to persuade people to take up smoking. In particular, they have concentrated on creating new demand for their products among people who live in poorer countries that have not banned tobacco advertising, such as India and China (see pages 46–47).

Sports sponsorship

One of the most effective ways that the tobacco companies keep their name in the public eye is by sponsoring sports events. Big companies donate huge sums of money to popular events such as grand prix racing, stock car racing, and snooker. In return, they get their brands and logos seen on TV screens around the world.

The European Union is in the process of banning all tobacco-related **sponsorship** of sport because it believes that it encourages people to take up smoking. However, many people believe that this will not be the end of tobacco-related sponsorship. They say that big sporting events may simply move to countries where bans do not exist.

Viewpoints

Sports sponsorship by tobacco companies is being made illegal in many countries. But not everyone thinks the ban is necessary.

- ## Sports sponsorship by tobacco companies should be banned

Tobacco advertising on TV is banned in many countries. But by sponsoring popular sporting events, giant tobacco companies are able to promote their products and advertise their brands on TV screens all around the world. They are also linking their brand names with exciting sports and sending out a message that it's cool to smoke.

- ## Sports sponsorship by tobacco companies is OK

If the tobacco companies have so much money, why shouldn't they spend some of it on supporting sporting events? People watching these events concentrate on the sport itself and are not influenced by whoever is sponsoring it.

What do you think?

Getting hooked

People start smoking for many different reasons, but the reason that most people continue to smoke is that they are **addicted** to the **nicotine** in tobacco. When someone is hooked on nicotine, their body and their mind come to rely on the drug for its effects.

How nicotine works

As soon as nicotine reaches the brain, it causes the release of a natural chemical called **dopamine**. Dopamine raises the smoker's heart rate and **blood pressure**, and also creates a feeling of pleasure. However, when the **stimulus** of nicotine wears off, those feelings of pleasure disappear. The smoker then wants another cigarette, as both their body and their mind **crave** the sensations produced by the drug. This is how someone becomes both physically addicted to and **psychologically dependent** on nicotine.

Physical addiction

Physical addiction happens when people become used to having a certain amount of nicotine in their blood. When that level drops, they experience unpleasant **withdrawal symptoms**, and start to feel restless, anxious, and irritable. At this stage, most people reach for another cigarette to top up the nicotine levels in their blood.

▌When smokers are stressed out, they crave a cigarette to calm them down. The only trouble is, it doesn't work for long!

Question

How long does it take to become addicted to nicotine?

Psychological dependence

At the same time as smokers' bodies are becoming physically addicted to nicotine, they are also developing psychological dependence on the drug. When someone is psychologically dependent on a drug, they depend or rely on it because of the way it affects their emotions or moods. They feel that they cannot cope without it.

Needing more

Nicotine addiction doesn't just make someone want another cigarette – it makes them want more and more. A smoker's brain soon becomes accustomed to the stimulus of nicotine, and requires a larger dose of the drug in order to produce the same release of dopamine as before. So smokers need to take in larger amounts of nicotine to achieve the same sensation they had when they first started smoking.

Desperate for a smoke

Some heavy smokers become so dependent on tobacco that they try to avoid any situation where they will be forced to go without a cigarette for a long time. A few smokers even stay away from restaurants where smoking is not allowed, or turn down invitations to go to the cinema. Some very heavy smokers suffer **panic attacks** if they have to stay for a long while in a place where smoking is strictly not allowed.

Answer

Nicotine addiction happens very quickly. People usually start craving more nicotine after they have smoked only two or three times.

A smoker's day

For most heavy smokers, a cigarette is the first thing they think about when they wake up in the morning, and their whole day is ruled by their need for tobacco. This pattern can develop very soon after someone takes up smoking.

❗ The first cigarette of the day

At least one in ten of all smokers have their first cigarette within fifteen minutes of waking up.

A bad start

All heavy smokers wake up in the morning with their mouth and tongue coated with stale smoke. As they try to clear their lungs, they often have a coughing and wheezing fit. But in spite of the awful taste in their mouth, and the fact that they feel so bad, they are already beginning to think about their first smoke of the day. Many smokers don't even make it out of bed before they reach for their first cigarette.

Problems at work

Throughout their working day, heavy smokers are thinking about when they can have their next smoking break. This makes it very hard for them to concentrate on work. As the break approaches, they begin to think more and more longingly about their next cigarette. If they are unable to take regular breaks, they become restless and irritable.

Most workplaces today operate a no-smoking policy, so taking a smoking break will often involve going outside the building to huddle on a fire-escape or in a draughty doorway – not a very enjoyable experience!

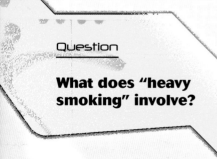

Question

What does "heavy smoking" involve?

Winding down?

For a heavy smoker, evenings are seen as an opportunity for more smoking, and meals may be hurried. One of the worst nightmares for a heavy smoker is running out of cigarettes after the shops have closed. Heavy smokers will know all the places where they can go for a late-night supply.

I Smoking doesn't seem glamorous when people have to take smoking breaks in the rain like this.

Smokers may go to bed determined to quit their habit in the morning. But the next day, the same unrelenting cycle begins again.

This couldn't be me?

When young smokers look at the lifestyle of heavy smokers, they simply cannot imagine that they would ever get like that. But many young smokers find that they are falling into exactly the same pattern. Very soon after people first take up smoking, they find that they are constantly on the lookout for opportunities to smoke. Would you ever want your life to be ruled by cigarettes?

Answer

Heavy smoking is often defined as anything more than twenty cigarettes a day. But even five cigarettes a day can seriously damage a person's health.

What does tobacco do?

Tobacco has short-term and long-term effects on the body. Its immediate effects can seem quite pleasant, but new smokers soon start to feel the bad effects. As well as feeling much less fit, the new smoker will start to smell of smoke and to look less good as well. However, all the bad effects can disappear very fast – once someone stops using tobacco.

Immediate effects

When smokers **inhale** tobacco smoke into their lungs, a range of different things happen inside their body. The **nicotine** causes their heart to beat faster, and their **blood pressure** is raised. Nicotine also triggers the release of **dopamine** in the brain, creating a brief sense of relaxation and calm.

❚ Smokers often become depressed and demoralized, and this is reflected in the way they look.

At the same time, however, the tobacco smoke irritates the lining of the nose, throat, and lungs. This makes the smoker produce extra mucus and often makes them start to cough. For many people whose bodies have not become accustomed to the effects of tobacco, smoking also makes them feel sick and dizzy.

Short-term effects

After someone has been smoking for a few weeks more symptoms appear. Smokers begin to develop an irritating and persistent cough. They may find that they get breathless easily, feel less fit, and lack energy. Smokers find it hard to fight off bugs and viruses and frequently suffer from bad colds. Also, because a smoker's lungs are coated with **tar**, a simple cold can often turn into a serious chest infection.

Body changes

Smoking can also change a person's body shape, making them less healthy and attractive than before. Because nicotine suppresses appetite, some smokers stop eating properly, and experience unhealthy weight loss. Other smokers find that their bodies are storing fat in unusual places. Heavy smokers usually store fat around their waist and upper body, causing an imbalance in the waist to hip measurement (WHR), which is a measure of overall health. People with a high WHR run a greater risk of developing high blood pressure, heart disease, diabetes, and some forms of cancer.

"I'd only been smoking for a few weeks, but I could definitely feel my body changing. I just didn't look so good – and I felt horrible in the mornings. I decided it definitely wasn't worth it."

Sophie, a teenager who decided to give up smoking

Bad smells

One of the most obvious ways that smoking affects people is that it immediately makes them smell disgusting. The smell of stale cigarette smoke clings to smokers' hair, skin, and clothes, and lingers in the air around them.

Skin and teeth

Smokers often find that their skin looks pasty and unhealthy. Tobacco affects a smoker's skin in two ways. First of all, smoke acts on the skin from the outside, drying out its surface and leaving it feeling itchy and parched. Secondly, tobacco restricts the flow of blood to the skin, so it acquires a greyish, wasted appearance. When compared with healthy skin, a smoker's skin has less elastin (the substance that keeps it soft and supple) and less vitamin A. As a result, regular smokers in their forties often have as many wrinkles on their face as non-smokers in their sixties.

"I had one date with a girl who smoked. Her breath smelled disgusting – and so did her hair and clothes. Only a loser would want to kiss an ashtray!"

Jake, a non-smoker aged sixteen

As well as damaging a smoker's skin, tobacco also stains it yellowish-brown. Many heavy smokers have permanently stained fingers and some have stains around their mouths. Tobacco also stains a smoker's teeth, leaving unsightly dark brown patches.

Not just smokers

People who use **chew** or **dip** tobacco also start to look and feel unhealthy as the chemicals in tobacco spread throughout their body. They may develop painful **ulcers** inside their mouth or on their tongue. Their friends and family will also be aware that their breath smells disgusting, and that their teeth are becoming yellow and stained.

Giving up quickly

If someone manages to stop smoking at an early stage, all the bad effects of smoking will disappear very quickly. Within a few weeks, the person's lungs will be back to normal and they will be feeling and looking good again.

▌ Most heavy smokers look old before their time, with heavily lined, unhealthy-looking skin.

Chris's story

Chris had been a heavy smoker since he was 18, and by the age of 40 he looked as though he was 60. This fact was really brought home to Chris when he was recovering from having his leg amputated – a result of smoking-related problems with his **circulation**. Chris's brother Nick came to visit him in hospital. Recognizing the family likeness, a nurse greeted Nick and talked to him about his "father's" condition. Nick gently put the nurse right – he explained that in fact he wasn't Chris's son. He was his twin brother!

Smoking and sexual health

Smoking is linked to a number of sexual problems. It affects men's ability to have an erection, and also makes it harder for a couple to **conceive** a child. If a woman who smokes becomes pregnant, she faces the risk of losing her child. She also puts her unborn child at serious risk if she continues smoking while she is pregnant.

I The more a pregnant woman smokes, the smaller her baby is likely to be, and the more problems it is likely to develop.

Sexual problems

Smoking can be the cause of sexual problems between couples. Many people find the smell of smoke on their partner's breath, hair, and clothes unattractive. Surveys conducted among a group of men in their thirties and forties reveal that smoking increases the risk of male **impotence** (inability to get an erection) by as much as 50 per cent. The anti-smoking charity ASH has calculated that around 12,000 young men in the United Kingdom are impotent as a result of smoking.

Smoking and fertility

Smoking affects **fertility** in both men and women. Men who smoke produce fewer **sperm** than non-smokers and their **semen** contains a higher proportion of abnormal sperm. Women who smoke are also less fertile and usually take longer to conceive a child than non-smokers. Female smokers are also at risk from cancer of the cervix (the neck of the womb). This disease often results in the removal of the womb, ending any chance of becoming pregnant.

■ Babies of mothers who smoke are often seriously underweight and need special care in order to survive.

Smoking and pregnancy

It is not safe for a woman to smoke at all while she is pregnant. Smoking during pregnancy reduces the amount of oxygen reaching the growing baby. This can seriously affect the baby's growth. Women who smoke during pregnancy face the risk of miscarriage – losing their baby before it is fully grown. They also have an increased chance of having a baby that is dead when it is born, or one that dies soon afterwards. Most babies born to women who smoke are underweight. These children are also likely to remain small for their age throughout their childhood.

Smoking in pregnancy has been linked to a range of health problems in babies and children, including **cleft palates**, **asthma**, and digestive problems. The children of mothers who smoke heavily in pregnancy are also more likely to suffer from learning difficulties, such as poor concentration and problems with processing information.

🛈 Damage to unborn babies

When a pregnant woman smokes, most of the damage to her unborn baby occurs in the last six months of pregnancy. So pregnant women who give up smoking as early as possible are giving their child a better chance of a healthy future.

Tobacco is associated with over 50 diseases and disorders. There's no doubt about it – tobacco kills. Smoking causes more than three million early deaths each year, and most of those deaths are extremely painful. Every part of the body is poisoned by tobacco, but the most dramatic effects take place in the lungs, heart, and mouth.

Damaged lungs

As soon as smokers take their first breath of tobacco smoke, they begin the process of damaging their lungs. Healthy lungs are made up of pinkish, spongy tissue. But a smoker's lungs soon become hardened, discoloured, and rough in texture. This happens as they are burnt by smoke, coated with **tar**, and attacked by a poisonous mixture of chemicals.

Lung damage caused by smoking leads to coughing and breathlessness. It also results in many serious diseases, ranging from **asthma** and **bronchitis** to **emphysema** (a **chronic** disease that causes sufferers to struggle for every breath they take) and lung cancer.

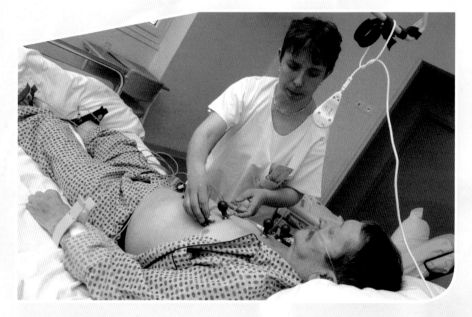

❚ By the time they reach their forties, many smokers are experiencing serious lung and heart problems.

Heart and circulation problems

Over time, smoking weakens the heart and the whole **circulation** system. **Nicotine** stimulates a smoker's heart to pump blood faster round the body, while the poisons in tobacco smoke have the effect of hardening veins and arteries and causing blood clots (lumps). Altogether, this puts a great strain on the heart and often leads to heart attacks or strokes.

Many smokers have poor circulation, and in some cases this problem becomes so severe that they have to have a limb amputated. Smoking affects the body's ability to heal wounds, and heavy smokers may also suffer from sores or **ulcers**.

❚ Chewing or smoking tobacco can lead to major gum disease.

Mouth, tongue, and throat

Smokers' mouths and throats are repeatedly filled with tobacco smoke – and this can have some gruesome effects. Many smokers' gums become decayed and bleeding, causing their teeth to wobble or even fall out, and some people develop painful ulcers in their mouths.

Some smokers may suffer from **oral cancer**. Oral cancer can attack the mouth, lips, gums, tongue, or jaw. It is extremely painful and can leave its victims unable to feed themselves or even talk. Pipe and cigar smokers and people who use **chew** or **dip** tobacco are especially likely to suffer from oral cancer.

❗ Chewing tobacco and oral cancer

A recent survey has shown that people who chew or dip tobacco are 50 times more likely to develop oral cancer than people who do not use tobacco.

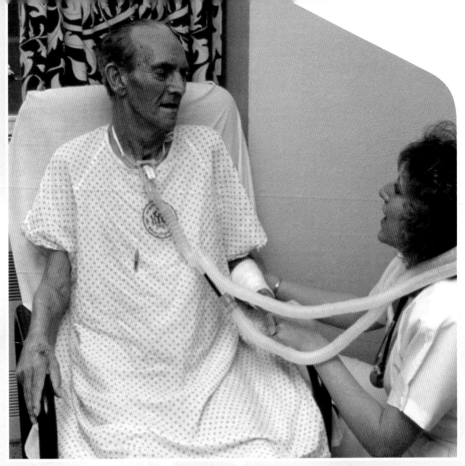

▌Smoking can literally take your breath away. Here, a lung cancer patient has to rely on a respirator to help him breathe.

The big killers

Most smoking-related deaths are caused by cancer. The most common types of cancer among tobacco users are cancer of the lungs, throat, and tongue. However, the **carcinogens** (cancer-causing substances) in tobacco travel all round the body in the bloodstream and can cause cancers in other organs, including the stomach, bladder, and kidneys. Women smokers also increase their risk of developing cancer of the breast or the womb.

After cancer, **bronchitis** and **emphysema** come a close second, while heart disease is also a major killer. A smoker is two to three times more likely to suffer a heart attack than a non-smoker.

⚠ Lives cut short

- One in two smokers will die from diseases related to smoking.

- Every cigarette a person smokes takes, on average, five minutes off their life.

- People killed by tobacco in middle age lose, on average, more than twenty years of life.

Apart from the pain of the diseases themselves, there is also the agony of surgery and other treatments. Surgery for **oral cancer** often involves the removal of the tongue or the jawbone. As one young tobacco-chewer put it, after his cancer surgery he was "the boy without a face".

John Diamond's story

The British journalist John Diamond had an apparently perfect life – a weekly column in a national newspaper, regular appearances on TV, a beautiful wife who was also a celebrity chef, and two young children. But he lost them all and his own life because of smoking. At the age of 43 John was diagnosed with throat cancer. Two months later, another **tumour** was discovered in his tongue and he had to undergo **radiation therapy**.

At around this point, John decided to make his story public. For the next four years, until his death at the age of 47, he wrote about his experiences in his newspaper column, made a TV film, and wrote a book. He also toured the country, talking to groups of young people and urging them not to make the same mistakes as him.

∎ John Diamond in 2001, looking painfully thin. He died a few months after this photo was taken.

John Diamond's story is shocking, but he told it with honesty and humour. In his book, he described having to wear a bib, drooling like a baby, and needing to be fed by a tube. He also related how he had to have an electronic voice-box fitted and how it made him sound like "a little old man called Albert". The lasting message of John Diamond's book is his sadness at throwing his future away – all because of a stupid habit.

Sooner or later, most smokers decide that it's time to quit. They may be worried about their health, their looks, or the amount of money they're throwing away. For most people, giving up tobacco isn't easy – but it can be done.

I Giving up smoking can give people the chance to enjoy playing sports again.

Time to stop

Most smokers think or talk about giving up several times a day! But it's much harder to do it than to think or talk about it. Once a smoker's body has become accustomed to the constant **stimulus** of **nicotine**, it's hard to do without it. There's no denying the fact that most long-term smokers find their first few weeks without tobacco a real struggle. But everyone who has managed to quit agrees that it's all worth it. Not only do they get an incredible sense of liberation once they have put their habit behind them, but they can also look forward to a much healthier and wealthier future.

Withdrawal symptoms

When people first stop smoking, they usually experience a range of **withdrawal symptoms**. The first and most noticeable of these is a powerful **craving** for tobacco. Cravings are usually especially strong at times when the smoker was used to having a cigarette – such as first thing in the morning or after a meal.

Doing without tobacco after a long period of physical **addiction** and **psychological dependence** can produce a number of reactions. People may be irritable and short-tempered, or feel restless or depressed. Some find it hard to concentrate, while others have trouble sleeping. Eventually, however, these symptoms disappear as the ex-smoker's body begins to function well again without the stimulus of nicotine.

▌Food tastes really good again once the effects of smoking have worn off.

Life after smoking

Once they have made it through the withdrawal period, ex-smokers usually begin to feel fantastic. They rediscover the pleasures of waking up in the morning feeling really well and refreshed. They start to enjoy the taste of food again, get their energy back, and look much better too.

In many cases, ex-smokers are so relieved to have got rid of their habit that they never touch tobacco again, but others struggle to shake off their addiction. Some find themselves returning to tobacco at times when their lives get difficult. However, once a smoker has experienced the freedom of life without tobacco, they are usually keen to try quitting again. At this stage, they often look around for help.

"Within a week of giving up smoking, I had stopped coughing. In two weeks I was able to run for the bus. The difference it made to my life was amazing!"

Sam, an office worker

Getting support

Fortunately, there is plenty of help available for people who are trying to give up tobacco. A number of organizations run telephone helplines, offering support and advice to people wanting to stop smoking. There are also websites to visit, books to read, and a range of products to buy – all designed to help people give up tobacco.

A helping hand

A large number of methods and treatments exist to help people give up smoking, including **hypnosis**, **acupuncture**, and **counselling**. Some people find it helpful to join a "quit smoking group" where they work out ways to beat their habit. These discussion groups often concentrate on finding other activities to replace smoking, such as chewing gum.

Positive thinking

Some of the best programmes for quitting smoking simply rely on the power of positive thinking. They appeal to people's desire to help themselves, and concentrate on the positive aspects of giving up tobacco – such as improved health and **self-esteem**. They also give people lots of encouragement in their efforts to quit.

▌For people struggling to give up smoking, there are telephone helplines to call, staffed by friendly, well-trained advisers.

Question

Is it worth giving up smoking, once you've got all that tobacco in your body?

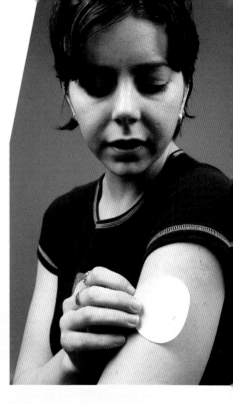

> *"No one should ever think it is too late to quit. Smoking isn't a one-way street ending in an inevitable death. People can take control and reduce the risks very substantially and very quickly by giving up at any age."*
>
> Clive Bates, director of the anti-smoking charity ASH (Action on Smoking and Health)

Nicotine substitutes

Once a smoker has decided to give up tobacco, the hardest problem they face is weaning their body off **nicotine**. Some people find it easier to do this slowly. A range of **nicotine substitutes** has been designed to provide ex-smokers with a supply of nicotine that can then be gradually reduced.

Nicotine substitutes include nicotine gum, lozenges, and skin patches. They all provide ex-smokers with the dose of nicotine their bodies have become accustomed to, but without the other poisons contained in tobacco. Obviously, this is not a long-term solution as regular doses of nicotine still have a harmful effect on the body, but some ex-smokers have found these products helpful in the process of giving up tobacco.

▌Skin patches like this are just one of the products that help to reduce the symptoms of withdrawal from nicotine.

Answer

Yes. Research has shown that even long-term smokers who quit dramatically reduce their chances of dying from tobacco-related diseases. The younger a person is when they stop, the better their chances are.

Smoking in society

Does smoking appeal more to certain groups in society than others? Surveys of smokers in **developed countries** all show definite patterns – and their results make worrying reading.

Rich and poor

Everyone has an image of the rich and powerful business tycoon puffing away on a fat cigar, but in fact this picture is not typical. Surveys show that the wealthy and well-educated members of our society are much less likely to smoke than people in the poorer social groups. People with fewer advantages may turn to smoking because they believe it will help them feel more relaxed and more able to deal with their problems. But, sadly, smoking brings problems of its own.

These patterns of smoking also have an impact on the health of the different social groups – there are almost twice as many smoking-related early deaths amongst the poorer members of our society.

> *"Industry efforts to target women are there for all to see. Since the introduction of Virginia Slims in 1968, there has been an explosion of female-only brands. From free introductory samples to the **sponsoring** of women's tennis, women are – as the industry says – under 'attack'."*
>
> Report on Women and Smoking, undertaken by ASH (Action on Smoking and Health) for the Cancer Research Campaign

Male and female

In the past, many more men than women used tobacco, but this pattern is changing in developed countries. Since the 1960s, the proportion of women smokers in developed countries has remained almost the same, while the percentage of male smokers has dropped dramatically. Nowadays, the numbers of adult male and female smokers are roughly equal. Among teenage girls, the smoking rate is rising quickly.

But what is the reason for this trend? One factor leading to the rise of young women smokers may be their increased spending-power and independence. But much of the blame for this trend can be laid at the door of the giant tobacco companies.

In recent years, tobacco companies have targeted much of their advertising at young women, in their efforts to get them to smoke. Their advertisements have conveyed a subtle message that smoking makes women seem sexy and sophisticated, and helps to keep them slim. Tobacco companies have also developed special products for women, such as "light" and "menthol" cigarettes. They have created packaging designed to attract young women and given their cigarettes appealing names like Vogue or Ultra-Slims.

Young and old

The most dramatic trend of all in smoking patterns is the increased number of teenage smokers. In the mid-1990s, rates of teenage smoking in developed countries began to climb steeply, with girls gradually overtaking boys. This worrying trend is discussed on pages 36–37.

▌ Smoking among young women is on the increase, but there are special health dangers for women who smoke. They are at greater risk from cancer of the breast and the womb and they are more likely to develop osteoporosis, a disease in which bones become very brittle.

Children become aware of cigarettes at a very early age – and many young people are tempted to give smoking a try. However, these early experiments do not necessarily lead on to regular smoking. Although smoking is a growing problem among teenagers, it is important to remember that most teenagers do not smoke.

Young people's health

Often, young people believe the dangers of smoking don't apply to them, but the medical evidence shows a very different picture. Children and teenagers who smoke are two to six times more likely than non-smokers to suffer from coughs, wheezing, and shortness of breath. Young smokers are also three times as likely to have time off school. A recent US survey found that smoking during the teenage years can cause permanent changes to the lungs that can increase the long-term risk of someone suffering from cancer.

Getting hooked young

Because young people have smaller bodies than adults, they can become **addicted** to **nicotine** very quickly. A UK survey of smokers aged 11 to 16 found they had the same levels of nicotine dependence as adults, with one-third of them lighting up within 30 minutes of waking up. Over

Question

Does the age at which someone starts smoking affect their later smoking habits?

half the teenage smokers questioned said they would find it very hard to go without cigarettes for a week.

Why do young smokers start?

One of the strongest factors influencing young people to take up smoking is their family's attitude to it. Children are three times more likely to smoke if both their parents smoke. Many young smokers are influenced by the smoking habits of their older brothers or sisters. Friends also play a very important part in encouraging each other to smoke.

Exposure to tobacco brands also plays a significant part in causing young people to take up smoking. Advertisements for tobacco, sports **sponsorship**, and positive images of smoking in films and on TV all help to persuade young people that smoking is cool.

∎ To some young people, smoking may seem glamorous and sophisticated. Are they really aware of what they're getting into, though?

Answer

Yes. The younger a person is when they start to smoke, the more likely they are to be a smoker for life. People who don't start smoking before they are twenty are unlikely to become smokers later in life.

Smoking isn't just a problem for smokers – it's an issue for everyone in society. Whenever smokers light up, they fill the air around them with tobacco smoke, forcing other people to become passive smokers. But what effect does **passive smoking** have on us all?

❗ Effects of passive smoking

Short-term exposure to tobacco smoke can cause:

- eye irritation
- headaches
- dizziness
- nausea
- coughing
- wheezing.

Long-term exposure to tobacco smoke can increase the risk of:

- cancer
- heart disease
- bronchitis
- pneumonia
- asthma
- middle-ear infections in children and infants
- cot deaths in babies.

What is passive smoking?

When people breathe in the smoke from others' cigarettes they are **inhaling** the same poisonous mixture that smokers take into their lungs. They are forced to inhale over 4,000 chemicals, including at least 40 known **carcinogens** (cancer-causing substances). Passive smokers also breathe in **carbon monoxide**, which affects the body's ability to deliver sufficient oxygen to organs such as the heart and the brain.

People who are forced to breathe in large quantities of others' smoke suffer from a range of symptoms, from sore eyes, headaches, and sore throats, to more serious complaints, such as **asthma** and **bronchitis**. They are also at risk from all the other diseases caused by smoking, including cancer.

Who suffers?

Anyone who has to spend time in a smoky environment is forced to become a passive smoker, but the people who live with smokers are most at risk. Amongst the members of a smoker's family their children are especially vulnerable. The very serious problem of children and passive smoking is discussed on pages 40–41.

Outside the home, smoking can cause a health hazard in public places. Many countries have banned smoking in offices and shops and on public transport, and some governments have banned smoking in restaurants and bars.

❚ When someone in the group decides to light up, they force everyone else to breathe their smoke too.

Heather's story

Heather Crowe had never smoked in her life, but she worked for many years as a waitress, serving in restaurants with smoking sections. When she went to her doctor feeling unwell, she was diagnosed with advanced lung cancer. Heather took her case to the courts to claim **compensation** for injury caused by second-hand smoke in the workplace. Heather won her case, and her claim was the first to be accepted by the Workplace Safety and Insurance Board of Ontario.

Living with a heavy smoker can be very hard – especially for the children in the family. As well as having to put up with the smoke and the smell, smokers' families also have to suffer the serious health effects of **passive smoking**.

"Even though my Dad never smokes inside our house, I still hate the fact that he's a smoker. It make me really sad that he gets out of breath and coughs all the time. Sometimes I have nightmares that he'll die before I grow up."

Kate, the daughter of a heavy smoker

▌Young children are at special risk from their parents' cigarette smoke – and they can't get away.

Nowhere to go

When a parent smokes indoors, the children cannot escape from the smoke. Babies and very young children cannot ask to leave a smoky room or car. Some children feel anxious about raising the subject and others may not be allowed to leave even if they ask.

Apart from the many health hazards, the families of heavy smokers have to put up with the constant smell of stale cigarette smoke. They also have to get used to living in a home that is scattered with ashtrays filled with old cigarette-ends and ash. Many children of smokers hate living in a smoky, smelly environment.

Children's health

All the chemicals in tobacco smoke have very bad effects on children's growing bodies. Many children living with smokers suffer from **bronchitis**, **pneumonia**, coughing and wheezing, **asthma** attacks, and ear infections – all caused by breathing in second-hand smoke.

Other problems

For many young people, seeing one or both their parents smoking leads them to see the habit as normal. They may decide that smoking is a perfectly acceptable thing to do – and start smoking themselves. Even if they are put off by their parents' smoking, simply having cigarettes around all the time can make it very hard to resist temptation.

However, not all children follow their parents' example. Instead, they may beg them to give up and become very worried about them. Many children of smokers feel sad that their parents are wrecking their health by smoking.

! Passive smoking and children

- Almost half the world's children live in households where at least one person smokes.

- Children of smokers are three times more likely to take up smoking than children from non-smoking families.

- Samples taken from the saliva of children growing up in a household where both parents smoke reveal that they are **inhaling** the equivalent of 80 cigarettes a year.

Our society pays a heavy price for the problems caused by tobacco – in terms of both money and human effort. There are also many personal costs for the smokers and their families. These include the greatest cost of all, when smokers die young, leaving their families to manage without them.

Medical expenses

Every year, millions of people die early because of smoking, and billions of pounds are spent on medical treatment for smoking-related diseases. Patients suffering from **chronic** diseases, such as heart failure or cancer, have to spend long periods in hospital, undergoing expensive treatment and operations, while people with less serious problems also need

Fire tragedy

At 1 a.m., fire fighters were called to a London family home that was engulfed in flames. They were too late to save the mother and three children, who were all trapped upstairs when the staircase collapsed. Only the father managed to get out. He later revealed that he had stayed up late, smoking. "I must have fallen asleep with a cigarette in my hand," he admitted.

medical care and treatment. Large sums are also spent in trying to help people give up smoking.

Fighting fires

Smokers are responsible for starting thousands of fires each year – resulting in tragic loss of life and damage to property. Careless smoking and dropped cigarettes are the most common cause of fires in the home. In very dry countries, such as Australia, smokers can cause enormous damage, as a carelessly abandoned cigarette can start a forest or bush fire that rages out of control for hundreds of miles.

Costs to industry

All over the world, industries are affected by the smoking habits of their employees. Workers who are **addicted** to tobacco need to take frequent "smoking breaks" from work. Furthermore, millions of working days are lost each year because of tobacco-related illnesses.

Money up in smoke

Anyone who has been smoking for a while knows that it is a very expensive habit. Someone who smokes twenty cigarettes a day spends over £1,600 per year on cigarettes – enough for a luxury holiday for two or a good laptop computer. It has been estimated that someone who starts smoking at sixteen and smokes twenty cigarettes a day will spend almost £100,000 on cigarettes over the course of their lifetime. All this money just goes up in smoke!

❚ Hundreds of lives are lost every year because of fires caused by dropped cigarettes.

Many countries have laws to control the use of tobacco. Governments have passed strict laws limiting the sale and advertising of cigarettes. There are also laws and guidelines on places where people are allowed to smoke.

▌A hard-hitting anti-smoking poster on a street in Beijing, China.

Advertisements and warnings

During the 1990s, most governments in **developed countries** took a firm stand against tobacco, banning TV and cinema commercials. They also insisted that all tobacco products should carry a clear health warning. These warnings usually cover a large area of the packet with hard-hitting statements such as "Smoking kills".

Limiting sales

Laws on selling tobacco aim to prevent the spread of smoking amongst young people. In the United Kingdom, no one under sixteen can buy tobacco products. Throughout the United States, it is against the law to sell tobacco to anyone under the age of eighteen and this age limit also applies in most Australian states.

Smoke-free areas

In many countries, smoking is banned on public transport and in public places, such as cinemas and airports. In Australia and the Republic of Ireland it is against the law to smoke in any workplace, while many other governments have issued clear non-smoking guidelines for employers to follow.

Taxes on smoking

All governments put high taxes on cigarettes and other tobacco products. They claim they need this money to help them deal with all the problems caused by smoking. They also say that making cigarettes more expensive helps to put people off smoking.

Not everyone agrees with this point of view. Many anti-smoking campaigners think this is not an effective way to persuade people not to smoke. They claim that people who are **addicted** to smoking will continue to buy tobacco, however expensive it is. They also say that raising the cost of cigarettes hits poor people hardest, because they are the ones who are most likely to smoke (see page 34).

Viewpoints

Recently, there have been moves to ban smoking in all pubs, bars, and restaurants as well as in all public places, but many smokers object to this.

- **There should be a total ban on smoking in public**
  Non-smokers should never have to breathe in other people's harmful smoke. Once smokers are forced to realize how anti-social and dangerous their habit is, more of them will give up smoking.

- **There should still be some smoking areas**
  If a ban is introduced in all pubs, bars, and restaurants, smokers will have nowhere to go to socialize in public. Smokers have rights, just like other citizens, and they shouldn't be punished just because they smoke.

What do you think?

Fifty years ago, business was booming for the giant tobacco companies. But now that many people in **developed countries** have discovered the real truth about tobacco, smoking among adults is generally declining. This means that the future of the tobacco companies is not so secure. To keep their profits high, they desperately need to find new customers. This has led them to target the world's most vulnerable people.

Targeting the poor

Since the 1970s, there has been a vast increase in the number of smokers in the poorer countries of the world, as the tobacco giants have tried to create new demand for their products in Africa, Asia, and Eastern Europe.

In the world's **developing countries** there are few restrictions on tobacco advertising and few governments can spare the money to educate their people about the dangers of smoking.

▌ Tobacco companies use giant billboards and other forms of advertising to make sure that their products have a very high profile in the developing world.

Many people willingly turn to smoking, thinking at first that it is something that will make their lives easier. However, smoking cigarettes quickly wrecks the health of people in poor communities. Without the level of medical care that smokers receive in developed countries, many people die very quickly from smoking-related diseases.

Dirty tricks

Within the developing world, the tobacco companies have used many clever tricks to encourage people to smoke. Companies run glamorous events to publicize their products and hand out free samples of cigarettes. Recently, companies in the developing world have been concentrating their efforts especially on young women, as far fewer of them smoke than men.

Mean employers

Almost three-quarters of the world's tobacco is grown in developing countries, where people are expected to work long hours for very low wages. Tobacco plantation workers are at risk from the poisonous **pesticides** sprayed on the plants. They also often suffer from green tobacco sickness (GTS), an illness caused by absorbing nicotine through the skin. GTS causes nausea, weakness, and dizziness, and affects the heart rate of its victims.

Free samples

In Sri Lanka, the tobacco company BAT (British American Tobacco) sponsored a "Golden Tones Disco", employing young women in shimmering golden saris to offer each young person entering the disco a free Benson and Hedges cigarette and a light, saying, "Go ahead, I want to see you smoke it now." Young women were allowed into the disco free of charge, but the young men had to pay.

Smoking in developing countries

- Of the estimated 1.25 billion (1.25 thousand million) smokers in the world, 800 million live in developing countries.

- China alone suffers almost a million deaths a year from tobacco, and this figure is likely to double by 2025.

There's no denying the fact that the tobacco companies are extremely powerful. But there are plenty of people who are prepared to stand up to them. There are also many individuals and organizations dedicated to the task of educating people about the dangers of smoking.

❚ Many celebrities have joined in the fight against the power of the tobacco industry. Here, film star Jackie Chan takes part in an anti-smoking campaign.

Raising awareness

All over the world, anti-smoking groups run campaigns to expose the way the tobacco industry works and to reveal the dangers of tobacco. Some groups issue fact sheets and create presentations for use in schools. Some campaigners try to persuade governments to take action to reduce the power of the tobacco industry. Other groups organize protests and petitions against the tobacco companies.

In **developed countries**, governments play an important part in informing the public about the dangers of smoking. They produce anti-smoking posters and make sure that packets carry clear health warnings. Many countries have a national "No smoking day", when campaign groups and governments combine to encourage people to quit smoking.

No smoking here!

Over the last twenty years, people in the developed world have become increasingly aware of the dangers of **passive smoking**. Hospitals and schools have long been smoke-free zones, and many employers operate a ban on smoking in the workplace. Many people ask their friends not to smoke inside their homes, and smokers themselves often choose not to smoke inside, especially if they have young children at home.

Legal battles

In recent years, people have started to challenge the power of the tobacco companies in the courts. One of the most famous of these cases was conducted in 1994 by the US state of Missouri. The state's lawyers claimed that tobacco advertisements broke Missouri's advertising laws. They said that the large tobacco companies targeted children and concealed the **addictive** nature of cigarettes. The tobacco companies lost the case and were forced to pay US$6.1 billion (US$6.1 thousand million) (£3,240 million). This money was used to pay for the medical treatment of people with smoking-related diseases, and to finance anti-smoking programmes. After this victory many other US states followed Missouri's example and won large sums from the tobacco industry.

Jesse Williams's story

In 1999, a jury ordered the US tobacco company Philip Morris to pay US$81 million (£43 million) as **compensation** to the family of Jesse Williams, a lifelong smoker who had died of lung cancer. The Williams family claimed that, for most of his life, Jesse Williams believed that the manufacturers would not sell a harmful product. After the trial, Williams's widow made the following public statement: "My husband had a dying wish. He wanted to make cigarette companies stop lying about the health problems of smokers."

Are there things that worry you about smoking and tobacco use? If there are – either now or in the future – there are lots of people and places you can contact. There are many organizations that offer help and advice on smoking-related problems. You can find out more information about people and places to contact on pages 54–55.

Someone to talk to

Sometimes it can be hard to talk to people you know about the things that are worrying you. You may want to discuss your concerns **in confidence**, knowing that whatever you say will not be passed on to anyone you know. You may also feel that you need some expert advice.

▌Sometimes it can really help to discuss your worries about smoking with a friend – and there are many other sources of support too.

Fortunately, there's an easy way to find somebody sympathetic to talk to. Several organizations have telephone helplines – phones that are staffed by specially trained advisers. These advisers will listen carefully to your concerns and questions and offer you advice and support. Helpline services are completely confidential – so nobody will give away any of your secrets.

You can find details of telephone helplines on pages 54–55 of this book. Some helplines are open 24 hours a day. This means you can call them any time – even if you have a problem in the middle of the night.

Finding out more

If you want to find out more about tobacco and the problems associated with it, you can start by contacting the organizations listed at the back of this book. Many of them have useful websites and some supply information packs. Some organizations have local branches, and they will also provide helpful links to people you can contact.

! Five good reasons

If your friends offer you a cigarette, do you think you'll be able to say no? Here are five good reasons you could give:

- you want to look good and smell good

- you want to stay healthy

- you want to save your money

- you don't want to end up hooked on tobacco

- you want to live longer.

It's up to you

Are you worried that other people will try to persuade you to take up smoking? No one can tell you what to do – and your friends will end up respecting you more if you stick up for yourself.

In the end it's up to you to make your own decision about smoking, and you need to think very hard about what it means to you.

Glossary

acupuncture treatment involving inserting fine needles into the skin at certain points on the body

addiction when a person is unable to manage without a drug, and finds it extremely hard to stop taking it

additives substances that are added to tobacco, such as preservatives and flavourings

asthma respiratory disease that causes shortness of breath and wheezing

billboard large board for advertisements or posters

blood pressure rate at which the heart pumps blood through the body

bronchitis inflammation of the airways

carbon monoxide poisonous gas found in tobacco smoke

carcinogen substance that has been proved to cause cancer

chew type of tobacco that is chewed and can cause oral cancer

chronic lasting a long time or constantly reoccurring

circulation movement of blood around the body

cleft palate split in the roof of the mouth

compensation money given to someone to make up for a loss, injury, or suffering

conceive become pregnant

condense turn from a gas into a liquid

counselling advice and guidance given to people to help resolve their problems

craving strong or uncontrollable need or longing

developed country rich industrialized country

developing country poor non-industrialized country that is trying to develop its industry and economy

dip type of tobacco that is chewed and can cause oral cancer

dopamine chemical in the brain that is associated with feelings of pleasure

emphysema serious lung disease that causes breathlessness

fertility ability to create babies

filter device at the end of a cigarette designed to remove some of the tar from cigarette smoke

hypnosis therapy that involves someone entering a relaxed sleep-like state in which their mind is open to suggestion and can be guided towards a desired outcome

impotence inability to get an erection

in confidence privately, without telling anyone else

inhale breathe in

media TV, cinema, magazines, and newspapers, and any other forms of mass communication

nicotine addictive drug found in all tobacco products

nicotine substitutes products such as patches, gum, and lozenges that provide ex-smokers with a controlled dose of nicotine, without the other harmful effects of tobacco smoke

oral cancer cancer that can attack the mouth, lips, gums, tongue, or jaw

panic attack sudden very strong feeling of anxiety, which makes a person's heart race

passive smoking breathing in smoke from other people's cigarettes, cigars, or pipes

pesticide chemical for killing insects

pneumonia inflammation of the lungs

preservative something that keeps a product fresh

psychological dependence when a person feels they need a drug to get through everyday life and cannot cope without it

radiation therapy treatment of a disease, especially cancer, with X-rays or other types of radiation

self-esteem good opinion of oneself

semen fluid produced by males that contains sperm

snuff powdered tobacco for sniffing

sperm male reproductive cells

sponsorship giving money to a person or organization to fund a project, activity, or event, sometimes in return for advertising

stimulant drug that speeds up the activity of the central nervous system, making people feel alert and full of energy

stimulus something that causes a particular response or reaction in an organ, such as the brain

tar harmful, brown sticky substance that is found in cigarette smoke

tumour abnormal growth or lump

ulcer open sore that heals very slowly

withdrawal symptoms unpleasant physical and mental feelings experienced during the process of giving up an addictive drug

Contacts and further information

There are a number of organizations worldwide that provide information and advice about tobacco use. Some have helpful websites, or provide information packs and leaflets, while others offer help and support over the phone.

Contacts in the UK

ASH (Action on Smoking and Health)
102 Clifton Street
London EC2A 4HW
Tel: 020 7739 5902
www.ash.org.uk
An anti-smoking organization that provides information on the tobacco industry and the effects of tobacco. ASH produces hard-hitting fact sheets and presentations on a wide range of tobacco-related topics.

Cancer Research UK
PO Box 123
Lincoln's Inn Fields
London WC2A 3PX
Tel: 020 7242 0200
www.cancerresearchuk.org
Provides information on cancer, its treatment, and causes, including facts on smoking and cancer.

DrugScope
32–36 Loman Street
London SE1 0EE
Tel: 020 7928 1211
www.drugscope.org.uk
A national drugs information agency with services that include a library, a wide range of publications, and a website.

FRANK
Tel: 0800 77 66 00
Email: frank@talktofrank.com
www.talktofrank.com
An organization for young people that gives free, confidential advice and information about drugs, including tobacco, 24 hours a day.

NHS Smoking Helpline
Tel: 0800 169 0 169
A helpline for people with smoking-related health problems, run by the National Health Service.

QUIT
Ground Floor
211 Old Street
London EC1V 9NR
Tel: 020 7251 1551
Quitline: 0800 00 22 00
www.quit.org.uk
An organization dedicated to helping people stop using tobacco. QUIT provides practical help and advice on how to stop smoking. It also runs two telephone helplines – Quitline and Asian Quitline.

Contacts in Australia and New Zealand

ASH Australia
PO Box 572
Kings Cross
Sydney
NSW 1340
Tel: 02 9334 1876
www.ashaust.org.au
An anti-smoking organization that provides information on the tobacco industry and the effects of tobacco. ASH produces hard-hitting fact sheets and presentations on a wide range of tobacco-related topics.

ASH New Zealand
Level 2
27 Gillies Avenue
Box 99 126
Newmarket
Auckland NZ
Tel: 64 9 520 4866
www.ash.org.nz
The New Zealand branch of ASH (see UK entry for more information about this organization).

Australian Council on Smoking and Health (ACOSH)
Level 1, 46 Ventnor Avenue
West Perth
WA 6005
Tel: 08 9212 4300
www.acosh.org
An organization dedicated to raising awareness about smoking and health issues.

The Cancer Council Australia
GPO Box 4708
Sydney
NSW 2001
Tel: 02 9036 3100
www.cancer.org.au
Provides information on cancer, its treatment, and causes, including facts on smoking and cancer.

QUIT NOW
Population Health Division
Australian Government Department of Health and Ageing
GPO Box 9848
Canberra
ACT 2601
Tel: 02 6289 1555
Quitline: 131 848
www.quitnow.info.au
QUIT NOW is run by the Australian National Tobacco Campaign. It supplies fact sheets about tobacco online and sends out information packs to help smokers quit their habit. It also has a telephone helpline.

Further reading

Dr Miriam Stoppard's Drug Information File: From Alcohol and Tobacco to Ecstasy and Heroin, by Miriam Stoppard (Dorling Kindersley, 1999)

Drugs, by Sarah Lennard-Brown (Hodder Wayland, 2001)

Drugs: The Truth, by Aidan Macfarlane and Ann McPherson (Oxford University Press, 2003)

It's Your Health: Smoking, by Judith Anderson (Franklin Watts, 2004)

Need to Know: Tobacco, by Sean Connolly (Heinemann Library, 2000)

Why do People Smoke?, by Jillian Powell (Hodder Wayland, 2000)

Why do People Take Drugs?, by Patsy Wescott (Hodder Wayland, 2000)

Further research

If you want to find out more about problems related to tobacco and smoking, you can search the Internet, using a search engine such as Google. Some useful keywords to try are:

Smoking + health
Passive smoking
Tobacco + cancer
Tobacco + addiction
Tobacco + law
Philip Morris case
Tobacco + developing world

Index